Guerrilla Marketing: Low-Cost Creative Strategies Outside of Digital

Copyright © 2024 Reginaldo Osnildo
All rights reserved.

PRESENTATION

INTRODUCTION TO GUERRILLA MARKETING

THE ART OF SURPRISE AND VISUAL IMPACT

POP-UP EVENTS: ORGANIZING TEMPORARY EVENTS IN UNEXPECTED LOCATIONS

AMBUSH MARKETING: TAKING ADVANTAGE OF LARGER OR COMPETITOR EVENTS TO CREATIVELY PROMOTE YOUR BRAND

GUERRILLA ADVERTISING IN URBAN SPACES

STICKERS AND GRAFFITI: TOOLS OF VISUAL IMPACT IN THE CITY

DISTRIBUTION OF CREATIVE GIFTS

FREE DEMONSTRATION AND SAMPLES IN UNUSUAL LOCATIONS

PARTNERSHIPS WITH LOCAL BUSINESSES

FLASH MOBS: ORGANIZING PERFORMANCES OR COLLECTIVE ACTIONS TO PROMOTE YOUR BRAND

INFILTRATION MARKETING: INTEGRATING YOUR PRODUCT OR SERVICE DISCREETLY INTO SPECIFIC COMMUNITIES OR GROUPS

ENVIRONMENTAL GUERRILLA CAMPAIGNS: CREATING FACILITIES THAT INTERACT WITH THE ENVIRONMENT IN UNEXPECTED WAYS

CUSTOM STREET ART

GUERRILLA ACTIONS AT EVENTS

URBAN PROJECTIONS

DISTRIBUTION OF GUERRILLA LITERATURE

CREATIVE POSTER CAMPAIGNS

GUERRILLA ACTIVATIONS IN PUBLIC SPACES

GUERRILLA ACTIONS WITH VEHICLES

GUERRILLA SENSORY MARKETING

ARTISTIC INTERVENTIONS

SEASONAL GUERRILLA MARKETING

WORD OF MOUTH AND GUERRILLA MARKETING

MEASURING SUCCESS IN GUERRILLA MARKETING

GUERRILLA ACTION PLAN

REGINALDO OSNILDO

PRESENTATION

Welcome to the universe where creativity and innovation meet to revolutionize the way your brand communicates outside the digital environment. " **Guerrilla Marketing: Low-Cost Creative Strategies Outside of Digital** " is more than just a book; is an invitation to embark on a journey to the heart of modern marketing, where big ideas don't depend on big budgets.

In this guide, you, the entrepreneur and marketer, will discover an arsenal of tactics and strategies designed to make your brand stand out in the physical market in a memorable and impactful way. With a focus on creativity, innovation, and the ability to make a big impact with limited resources, every page of this book is dedicated to providing practical ideas and valuable insights for running effective guerrilla marketing campaigns outside of the digital environment.

Why guerrilla marketing, you may ask? Because, in a world where consumers are bombarded with digital messages, creating a tangible and memorable connection can be the difference that puts your brand ahead. And this is where this book comes in, bringing my updated perception on traditional concepts, synthesizing the knowledge accumulated over years of marketing and innovating to adapt to today's challenges and opportunities.

From introducing guerrilla marketing to measuring the success of your campaigns, to engaging strategies like pop-up events, ambush marketing, advertising in urban spaces, distributing creative giveaways and more, each chapter is a step forward in your journey to win the attention and hearts of your audience in an unforgettable way.

This book is aimed at you who want to go beyond the conventional, exploring strategies that not only capture the attention of your target audience but also create a lasting brand experience. Throughout this guide, you will be constantly invited to reflect on how each idea can be adapted and implemented in your own business reality, ensuring that the proposed strategies are not only inspiring but also applicable.

Prepare to be inspired, challenged, and equipped with the tools you need to transform your brand into a notable force in the marketplace. The next chapter will introduce you to the fascinating world of guerrilla marketing, explaining its basic principles and how its effectiveness can be maximized outside of the digital environment. Are you ready to transform the ordinary into extraordinary? So, turn the page and start transforming your brand.

Yours sincerely

Reginaldo Osnildo

INTRODUCTION TO GUERRILLA MARKETING

At the heart of guerrilla marketing lies the essence of innovation and creativity. This chapter is your starting point in exploring non-digital strategies that can catapult your brand into the spotlight, even when operating with limited resources. You will discover here what defines guerrilla marketing, its importance and how it differs from traditional forms of marketing.

WHAT IS GUERRILLA MARKETING?

Guerrilla marketing is a marketing approach focused on using unconventional, creative and low-cost tactics to generate a big impact. Inspired by guerrilla tactics used in conflicts, where surprise and innovation trump brute force and large numbers, guerrilla marketing applies these principles in the business world. Your objective? Capture your audience's attention in unexpected ways, creating a lasting brand memory.

BECAUSE IT'S IMPORTANT?

In today's digital age, people's attention is a scarce and highly contested resource. Guerrilla marketing offers a refreshing alternative to saturated digital marketing approaches, allowing your brand to stand out in a unique way. Instead of competing for space in social media feeds or email inboxes, guerrilla marketing takes your message into the physical world, creating direct, memorable experiences with your audience.

DIFFERENTIATING FROM TRADITIONAL MARKETING

While traditional marketing often relies on substantial budgets for mass advertising and far-reaching campaigns, guerrilla marketing thrives on the art of doing more with less. It's intelligence, cunning and creativity that drives your campaigns, not the size of your budget. This approach allows small businesses and entrepreneurs to compete with market giants, offering a unique way to build brand awareness and customer loyalty.

HOW TO MAXIMIZE THE EFFECTIVENESS OF GUERRILLA MARKETING

To maximize the effectiveness of guerrilla marketing, you must:

- **Deeply know your target audience:** Understanding who they are, what they value, and how they live is fundamental to creating campaigns that resonate and surprise.

- **Be creative:** Think outside the box. Originality is the key to capturing attention and leaving a lasting impression.

- **Focus on impact, not budget:** Use resources wisely. A brilliant, well-executed idea is worth more than an expensive, uninspired campaign.

- **Measure success:** Learn from each campaign. Measure impact through audience feedback, media coverage, and any increase in brand visibility or sales.

PREPARING THE LAND

Before diving into specific guerrilla marketing strategies, it's vital to understand these basics. Each tactic you'll explore in the next chapters builds on these principles, challenging you to think differently about how to promote your brand.

Now that you're familiar with the basics of guerrilla marketing, it's time to explore how the art of surprise and visual impact can be used to capture your audience's attention. In the next chapter, we will discuss how the element of surprise and eye-catching visuals can be your greatest allies in creating memorable and effective marketing campaigns. Are you ready to spark your audience's curiosity and enthusiasm? So, go ahead and discover the power of surprise in guerrilla marketing.

THE ART OF SURPRISE AND VISUAL IMPACT

Surprise is one of the most powerful and memorable human emotions. In the context of guerrilla marketing, it becomes an invaluable tool, capable of transforming a simple message into an unforgettable experience for your audience. Combined with visual impact, the art of surprise can take your campaign to new heights, creating a strong emotional bond between your brand and your audience. This chapter explores how you can use these elements to capture people's attention and leave a lasting impression.

THE POWER OF SURPRISE

Surprise breaks the monotony of everyday life. It shocks, enchants and, above all, remains in people's memories. In guerrilla marketing, using surprise means creating unexpected moments that awaken emotions, making your brand remembered and discussed. But how do you create these moments? The key is to deeply understand your target audience and what they least expect but will deeply appreciate when confronted.

VISUAL IMPACT: MORE THAN A THOUSAND WORDS

Eye-catching visuals capture attention instantly. In an age of information overload, a powerful image can communicate your message quickly and effectively, creating an instant connection with your audience. Visual impact in guerrilla marketing can take many forms, from unusual art installations to creative use of urban spaces, ensuring your brand is noticed and remembered.

STRATEGIES TO MAXIMIZE SURPRISE AND VISUAL IMPACT

- **Unexpected events:** Organize actions or events in unusual places and times, where your audience does not expect a marketing intervention. This can range from an artistic performance in the middle of a public square to themed actions on unconventional dates.

- **Innovative visual installations:** Create installations that surprise with the creative use of space and the message.

Think about sculptures, projections, or any type of visual art that can be associated with your brand and that makes people stop to look and interact.

- Unusual ads: Use non-traditional advertising formats and spaces. It could be an ad in a completely unexpected place or a format that defies expectations, like a billboard that interacts with its surroundings.

- Flash mobs and performances: Harness the power of crowds to create a moment of surprise and delight. Flash mobs and artistic performances can generate a lot of attention and are perfect for sharing on social media, increasing the reach of your campaign.

SUCCESS STORIES

Including real examples of campaigns that have successfully utilized surprise and visual impact can inspire your own strategies. From simple actions like giving away free samples in a completely unexpected way, to complex brand-sponsored art installations, the element of surprise never fails to create a buzz.

Now that you understand the power of surprise and visual impact in guerrilla marketing, it's time to explore how these concepts can be expanded and deepened through pop-up events. In the next chapter, we'll discuss how hosting temporary events in unexpected locations can generate buzz, interaction, and a deep emotional connection with your audience. Get ready to discover how to transform ordinary locations into extraordinary settings for your brand. Let's go?

POP-UP EVENTS: ORGANIZING TEMPORARY EVENTS IN UNEXPECTED LOCATIONS

Pop-up events have become an invaluable marketing tool for brands looking to create a direct and memorable connection with their audience. These events, due to their temporary and often surprising nature, create a sense of urgency and exclusivity, attracting attention and generating conversations. This chapter explores how you can plan and execute effective pop-up events, turning unexpected locations into powerful marketing platforms for your brand.

THE ESSENCE OF POP-UP EVENTS

Pop-up events are temporary experiences that can take place almost anywhere, from an underutilized urban space to more traditional locations but with an innovative approach. The key element is surprise and exclusivity: consumers are attracted by the opportunity to participate in something unique that will not be available for a long time.

BENEFITS OF POP-UP EVENTS

- **Direct engagement:** Provide an opportunity to directly engage with your audience, allowing you to present your brand and products in an intimate and interactive way.

- **Buzz and media coverage:** Due to their innovative and often unusual nature, pop-up events tend to generate significant buzz, attracting local and even national media attention.

- **Market testing:** They are an excellent way to test new products, store concepts or markets without the commitment of a permanent presence.

PLANNING YOUR POP-UP EVENT

- **Define your goals:** Be clear about what you want to achieve with the pop-up event. Increase brand awareness? Launch a new product? Test a new market?

- **Choose the perfect location:** The location should surprise your target audience, but also be accessible and conducive to the type of experience you want to create.

- **Create a memorable experience:** Think beyond simply selling a product. Offer workshops, live presentations, or other interactive activities that engage attendees with your brand.

- **Promote your event:** Utilize all available channels - social media, local partnerships, and traditional media - to build anticipation and ensure a good turnout.

TIPS FOR SUCCESS

- **Innovation:** Always surprise. Use creativity to transform ordinary spaces into extraordinary experiences.

- **Flexibility:** Be prepared to adapt. The best pop-up events take advantage of opportunities and deal with unforeseen events quickly.

- **Customer focus:** The entire experience must be designed with the customer in mind. Their satisfaction and engagement with your brand are the true measures of success.

Pop-up events are just one of the many tactics you can use to create an effective guerrilla marketing campaign. In the next chapter, we'll dive into the world of ambush marketing, exploring how you can leverage larger events or the presence of competitors to promote your brand in a creative and impactful way. Be ready to discover how to turn competition and big events into unique opportunities for your brand to shine. Here we go?

AMBUSH MARKETING: TAKING ADVANTAGE OF LARGER OR COMPETITOR EVENTS TO CREATIVELY PROMOTE YOUR BRAND

Ambush marketing is a bold and intelligent strategy that is based on associating your brand with a highly visible event, product or service, without necessarily having an official partnership. This chapter will guide you through the principles of ambush marketing, showing you how you can utilize larger events or the presence of competitors to create a competitive advantage, increasing your brand's visibility in innovative and often surprising ways.

UNDERSTANDING AMBUSH MARKETING

Ambush marketing involves strategic positioning and creativity to take advantage of the attention generated by already established events or products. The key is to associate your brand with these opportunities in a way that feels natural but doesn't infringe on sponsorship rights or intellectual property. When executed well, this type of marketing can generate great visibility and discussion around your brand.

BENEFITS OF AMBUSH MARKETING

- **Cost-effectiveness:** Leveraging an existing event allows you to benefit from the visibility and buzz it generates, without the costs associated with official sponsorship.

- **Increased visibility:** By positioning your brand close to major events or competitions, you benefit from great media coverage and public interest in these events.

- **Creativity and innovation:** This approach challenges you to think creatively to connect your brand to large-scale events in an innovative and memorable way.

HOW TO IMPLEMENT AN AMBUSH MARKETING STRATEGY

- **Identify opportunities:** Keep an eye on upcoming events, product launches or competitor activities that may be relevant to your brand and target audience.

- **Plan carefully:** Develop a detailed plan for how you will take advantage of this opportunity. This may involve on-site promotional actions, social media campaigns or creative partnerships.

- Respect laws and guidelines: It is crucial to understand and respect intellectual property laws and sponsorship rights to avoid legal action.

- Measure impact: Establish clear metrics to evaluate the success of your ambush marketing campaign, such as increased visibility, social media engagement, or sales growth.

ETHICAL CONSIDERATIONS

Ambush marketing navigates a gray area between creatively seizing opportunities and potentially violating sponsorship rights. It is essential to approach these campaigns sensitively and ethically, ensuring that your strategy strengthens your brand image without causing unnecessary conflicts.

Now that we've explored how to use larger events and the presence of competitors to your advantage, it's time to look at your surroundings in a new way. In the next chapter, we'll discuss how to innovatively utilize urban public spaces for advertisements and installations that not only capture attention, but also delight and surprise your audience. Get ready to discover the limitless potential of urban spaces in creating memorable guerrilla marketing campaigns.

GUERRILLA ADVERTISING IN URBAN SPACES

Using the urban environment as a stage for your guerrilla marketing campaigns is an effective way to attract attention and leave a lasting impression on your audience. This chapter explores how you can transform ordinary public spaces into extraordinary brand experiences, using creativity and innovation to overcome budget constraints and make a big impact.

TAKING ADVANTAGE OF URBAN SPACE

The urban landscape is rife with opportunities for guerrilla marketing campaigns. From parks and public squares to busy city streets, these spaces provide a dynamic backdrop for creative advertising. The key is to look beyond the conventional use of these spaces, identifying unique ways to incorporate your brand into the urban landscape.

STRATEGIES TO IMPACT

- **Art installations and sculptures:** Create temporary installations that not only capture attention but also encourage interaction and sharing on social media.

- **Floor and wall advertisements:** Use street paintings, projections and stickers in high-traffic locations to surprise people during their daily routine.

- **Interactive actions in public spaces:** Promote interactive activities, such as games or exhibitions, that directly engage the public, offering them an unforgettable experience.

- **Guerrilla green:** Integrate natural elements into your campaigns, such as temporary gardens or environmental messages, to highlight your brand and raise awareness.

PLANNING AND EXECUTION

- **Know the rules:** Before launching your campaign, familiarize yourself with local regulations to avoid legal problems. You will often need to obtain permissions to use public spaces.

- **Focus on message:** Make sure your campaign clearly communicates your brand message, creating a direct connection between the action and the values you represent.

- **Safety and accessibility:** Plan your action ensuring that it is safe and accessible to all audiences, avoiding any potential nuisance or inconvenience to the community.

MEASURING SUCCESS

The impact of guerrilla advertising campaigns in urban spaces can be measured in a number of ways, including increased brand awareness, media coverage generated, social media engagement and direct audience feedback. Establish clear metrics before launching your campaign so you can objectively evaluate its success.

With the exploration of guerrilla advertising in urban spaces complete, it's time to delve deeper into specific tools that can be used to leave a visual mark on the city. In the next chapter, we'll delve into the world of stickers and graffiti, examining how these forms of artistic expression can be used to promote your brand in an indelible way. Ready to explore the potential of these creative tools? Let's move forward and find out how they can be integrated into your guerrilla marketing strategy.

STICKERS AND GRAFFITI: TOOLS OF VISUAL IMPACT IN THE CITY

In a world where traditional advertising often goes unnoticed, stickers and graffiti are emerging as powerful and creative forms of guerrilla marketing. This chapter explores how these two forms of expression can be used to create a strong presence for your brand in the urban fabric, generating discussions, increasing visibility and connecting with the public in an authentic and memorable way.

STICKERS: STICKER MESSAGES WITH GREAT POTENTIAL

Stickers are a low-cost but highly effective form of advertising that can be implemented in almost any urban environment. They give you the flexibility to deliver your message in unexpected places, capturing your audience's attention in surprising ways.

Strategies for effective use of stickers:

- **Attractive design:** Invest in a design that stands out, whether for aesthetics, message or some interactive element.

- **Strategic location:** Choose locations where your target audience is most likely to see and interact with your stickers. Think about high-traffic areas like shopping centers, coffee shops, universities, and public transportation.

- **Clear and concise message:** Given space limitations, your message must be direct but creative, encouraging whoever sees it to seek more information.

GRAFFITI: URBAN ART AS A BRAND VEHICLE

Graffiti is a powerful artistic expression, capable of transforming urban spaces and communicating messages in an impactful way. When used in a marketing strategy, it can not only increase brand visibility, but also add cultural and social value, aligning the company's image with contemporary values of creativity and urban expression.

Implementing graphite into your strategy:

- **Collaboration with local artists:** Establish partnerships with recognized graffiti artists and street artists who share your brand's values. This ensures authenticity and respect within the artistic community and the general public.

- **Careful location selection:** Identify cool, art-friendly spaces that are visible and accessible to your target audience.

- **Integration with the brand message:** Graffiti must tell a story that connects with the essence of your brand, creating an engaging visual narrative.

LEGAL AND ETHICAL CONSIDERATIONS

When implementing campaigns that use stickers and graffiti, it is crucial to consider legal and ethical aspects. Respect public and private property, obtain necessary permits, and ensure your campaign contributes positively to the urban environment and community.

MEASURING IMPACT

The success of sticker and graffiti-based campaigns can be measured through social media engagement, media coverage, community feedback and increased brand awareness. Establish specific metrics to evaluate the effectiveness of your strategy.

After exploring the potential of stickers and graffiti to create a strong visual brand in the city, the next chapter delves into the universe of creative gifts. We will discover how innovative and memorable promotional items can be used to strengthen your brand presence and establish a lasting emotional connection with your audience. Get ready to expand your guerrilla marketing strategy with giveaways that people will love so much they not only want it, but share it too. Let's go ahead?

DISTRIBUTION OF CREATIVE GIFTS

Creative giveaways are an effective way to leave a lasting impression on the minds of your audience. By offering something tangible, useful and, above all, memorable, you can increase brand awareness, generate goodwill and encourage positive word of mouth. This chapter explores how to develop and implement a stand-out giveaway strategy, capturing the essence of guerrilla marketing while creating meaningful connections with your audience.

THE POWER OF CREATIVE GIFTS

Gifts are not just souvenirs; They are engagement tools that carry your brand's identity into people's everyday lives. When well planned, they can be an extension of your marketing campaign, reinforcing the brand's message and increasing its visibility.

STRATEGIES FOR UNFORGETTABLE GIFTS

- **Originality:** Choose gifts that stand out for their design, functionality or a touch of humor. The goal is to create something that people want to use, show and share.

- **Brand alignment:** Make sure the gift reflects your brand's values and aesthetics. Each item distributed should be a tangible representation of what your brand stands for.

- **Utility:** Useful gifts have a longer shelf life and, consequently, keep your brand in the consumer's mind for longer. Think about items that can be integrated into the daily lives of your target audience.

- **Element of surprise:** The distribution of gifts must be as creative as the items themselves. Consider unusual packaging or delivery methods that create a memorable experience.

IDEAS FOR CREATIVE GIFTS

- **Eco-friendly products:** Sustainable items not only demonstrate the brand's social responsibility, but are also valued by the conscious public.

- **Technology and innovation:** Small gadgets or technological accessories with your brand logo can be both useful and impressive.

- **Personalization:** Personalized items create an emotional connection, making the recipient feel special and more likely to share their positive experience with others.

IMPLEMENTATION AND DISTRIBUTION

- **Events and fairs:** Take advantage of events relevant to your target audience to distribute your giveaways, creating a buzz around your presence.

- **Guerrilla actions:** Consider distributing gifts unexpectedly in public places, creating a pleasant surprise that will be associated with your brand.

- **Social networks:** Use social networks to promote the distribution of gifts, encouraging participation in contests or sharing campaigns.

MEASURING SUCCESS

The impact of creative giveaways can be measured through social media engagement, increased brand awareness, direct audience feedback and, ultimately, increased sales or inquiries. It is important to monitor these indicators to understand the return on investment.

After exploring how creative giveaways can be a powerful guerrilla marketing tool, the next chapter takes us on a journey into holding demonstrations and free samples in unusual locations. Discover how these tactics can create memorable experiences with your product, generating excitement and brand loyalty. Get ready to dive into strategies that not only showcase your product, but also delight and surprise your audience. Here we go?

FREE DEMONSTRATION AND SAMPLES IN UNUSUAL LOCATIONS

Creating an unforgettable experience around your brand often involves going beyond the conventional, especially when it comes to demonstrating your product or service. Offering free demonstrations and samples in unusual locations can capture your audience's imagination, generating not only interest but also a strong memory of your brand. This chapter explores how these tactics can be used effectively to engage your target audience in creative and impactful ways.

THE IMPORTANCE OF DIRECT EXPERIENCE

Free demos and samples allow potential customers to try your product directly, creating an immediate, tangible connection. When held in unusual locations or in an unexpected manner, these experiences become not only a proving opportunity but also a memorable event associated with your brand.

CHOOSING UNUSUAL LOCATIONS

The key to the success of these initiatives is the choice of location. Unusual places capture attention and generate curiosity, making the experience of discovering your product exciting. Think about places where your target audience is already present, but that are not traditionally used for marketing promotions, such as parks, cultural events, or even abandoned locations transformed for the event.

STRATEGIES FOR SUCCESSFUL EXECUTION

- **Contextualization:** Make sure the chosen location and distribution method make sense for the product or service you are promoting. The experience should feel authentic and not forced.

- **Interactivity:** Take the opportunity to interact directly with your audience. Use demos as a way to educate consumers about your product by highlighting its benefits in an engaging way.

- **Element of surprise:** Surprise is a powerful component of guerrilla marketing. Organize your actions so that the demonstrations and distribution of samples are a pleasant surprise for those who encounter them.

- **Cross promotion:** Use social media to expand the reach of your action, encouraging participants to share their experiences online. This could include specific hashtags, augmented reality filters, or contests.

MEASURING IMPACT

The success of these actions can be measured by increased brand recognition, engagement on social media, direct feedback from participants and, of course, impact on sales. It is important to collect data and feedback to understand what worked and what can be improved in future actions.

SUCESS HISTORIES

Include case studies or examples of brands that have managed to generate significant buzz and positive results by holding demos and giving away free samples in unusual locations. These stories can serve as inspiration and offer valuable insights for your own strategies.

With a deeper understanding of how demos and free samples in unusual locations can elevate your brand awareness, it's time to explore other creative collaborations. In the next chapter, we'll discuss how partnerships with local businesses can benefit your brand by offering new channels to reach your audience and build a community around your products or services. Join us to discover how these collaborations can be a win-win for everyone involved. Let's go?

PARTNERSHIPS WITH LOCAL BUSINESSES

Collaborating with local businesses opens up a range of opportunities for brands looking to take root in the community and expand their reach in an authentic and meaningful way. This chapter highlights the importance of these partnerships, offering strategies for creating synergies with local businesses, which can lead to increased visibility, enhanced brand image and development of a loyal customer base.

THE STRENGTH OF COMMUNITY

Partnerships with local businesses allow your brand to become part of the social and economic fabric of the community. These collaborations can range from joint promotions to shared events, leveraging local market knowledge and existing customer base to drive mutually beneficial impact.

STRATEGIES FOR EFFECTIVE PARTNERSHIPS

- **Identify partners aligned with your brand:** Look for businesses whose values and target audience complement yours. Synergy between the brands is crucial to the success of the partnership.

- **Create joint offers:** Develop promotions, products or services that combine the best of both businesses. This could include special bundles, cross-discounts, or exclusive products created in collaboration.

- **Organize shared events:** Use the physical space of each business to hold events that attract both audiences, such as workshops, lectures or product demonstrations.

- **Promote each other:** Use all available communication channels (social networks, websites, email marketing) to promote the partnership and your joint activities, maximizing exposure for both businesses.

BENEFITS OF LOCAL PARTNERSHIPS

- **Expanded audience access:** Reach new customer segments

that may be difficult to engage through other means.

- **Reinforcement of trust and credibility:** Association with established and respected businesses in the community can increase trust in your brand.

- **Resource optimization:** Sharing resources for promotions or events can reduce costs and increase ROI for both parties.

CONSIDERATIONS FOR SUCCESS

- **Clear communication:** Maintain open and clear lines of communication with your partner to ensure you are both aligned on goals and expectations.

- **Mutual commitment:** Success requires investment and commitment from both sides. Make sure each party is contributing fairly to the partnership.

- **Measure and adjust:** Establish metrics to evaluate the success of the partnership and be willing to make adjustments as necessary to optimize results.

After exploring the potential of partnerships with local businesses, our next step will be to delve into the world of flash mobs. In the next chapter, you will discover how organizing performances or collective actions can not only capture the public's attention in a dramatic way, but also create moments of joy and surprise that positively associate your brand in the minds of consumers. Get ready to unlock the power of flash mobs in guerrilla marketing. Here we go?

FLASH MOBS: ORGANIZING PERFORMANCES OR COLLECTIVE ACTIONS TO PROMOTE YOUR BRAND

Flash mobs are a vibrant and memorable expression of guerrilla marketing, bringing together groups of people to carry out an unexpected action, be it a dance, an artistic performance or a peaceful demonstration, in public places. These collective actions not only capture the public's attention in a dramatic way, but also create moments of surprise and joy, generating conversations and shares that can significantly increase your brand's visibility.

THE ESSENCE OF FLASH MOB

The essence of a flash mob lies in its ability to surprise and delight the public, transforming the ordinary into extraordinary. When executed well, flash mobs not only entertain but also convey powerful messages in a playful and engaging way, making them an effective tool for promoting your brand and values.

PLANNING A SUCCESSFUL FLASH MOB

- **Define your goal:** Whether it's promoting a product, raising awareness about a cause, or simply generating buzz around your brand, have a clear goal in mind.

- **Choose the location:** Locations with high visibility and traffic, such as public squares, transport stations and shopping centers, are ideal. Consider logistics and obtain necessary permits.

- **Develop the performance:** The action must be captivating and reflect the message you want to convey. Collaborating with artists, dancers or actors can help create a memorable performance.

- **Recruit participants:** In addition to professionals, you can involve the local community or brand followers to participate, increasing engagement and a sense of belonging.

- **Promote and share:** Use social media to tease and build anticipation before the event, and be sure to capture the performance on video for later sharing.

IMPORTANT CONSIDERATIONS

- **Respect for the public and the space:** Ensure that your action does not cause inconvenience or discomfort to the public and the space used.

- **Audience reaction:** Be prepared for different reactions and have a plan to positively engage with the audience during and after the event.

- **Legal aspects:** Check local regulations regarding public gatherings and obtain all necessary authorizations.

MEASURING IMPACT

The success of a flash mob can be measured by social media engagement, media coverage, increased brand awareness and audience feedback. Evaluate the scope of your action and alignment with established brand objectives.

After exploring how flash mobs can be used to create a strong impression and public engagement, the next chapter will look at infiltration marketing. You'll learn how to discreetly integrate your product or service into specific communities or groups, building authenticity and trust without seeming intrusive. Be ready to dive into marketing techniques that allow your brand to become a natural part of the conversation. Let's go ahead?

INFILTRATION MARKETING: INTEGRATING YOUR PRODUCT OR SERVICE DISCREETLY INTO SPECIFIC COMMUNITIES OR GROUPS

Infiltration marketing is a subtle but powerful strategy that involves discreetly inserting your brand into specific communities or groups so that it becomes part of the conversation without seeming forced or intrusive. This chapter discusses how you can use this approach to build authenticity, trust, and eventually brand loyalty while remaining respectful and relevant to your target audience.

UNDERSTANDING INFILTRATION MARKETING

Unlike more direct tactics, infiltration marketing focuses on creating organic relationships with potential customers by genuinely engaging with their communities. The key is to offer real and relevant value, whether through content, participation in discussions or support for events and causes important to the group.

STEPS TO AN EFFECTIVE INFILTRATION STRATEGY

- **Community research and selection:** Identify communities, online forums, social media groups or events that align with your brand values and where your target audience is active.

- **Understand the culture:** Before attempting infiltration, it is crucial to understand the culture, language and values of the group. This requires time and observation to ensure your brand can integrate authentically.

- **Genuine contribution:** Offer contributions that enrich the community. This could be in the form of valuable insights, relevant content, or support for community causes. The focus should be on adding value, not explicitly promoting your brand.

- **Build relationships:** Engage meaningfully with community members. Answer questions, participate in discussions, and be present as an active, contributing member.

- **Measure and adjust:** Track the impact of your infiltration strategy and be ready to adjust your tactics based on community feedback and responsiveness.

BENEFITS OF INFILTRATION MARKETING

- **Authenticity and trust:** By becoming a respected member of the community, your brand gains authenticity and creates a level of trust that is difficult to achieve through traditional marketing tactics.

- **Brand loyalty:** Genuine contributions and authentic relationships can convert community members into loyal advocates for your brand.

- **Valuable insights:** Immersing yourself in communities gives you a deep understanding of your target audience's needs and wants, allowing you to refine your offering and communication.

ETHICAL CONSIDERATIONS

It is crucial to approach infiltration marketing ethically and respectfully. Avoid any form of misrepresentation about your identity or intentions, and ensure that your participation adds genuine value to the community.

After exploring the nuances of infiltration marketing, the next chapter will reveal how to create environmental guerrilla campaigns. Discover how to use the environment in unexpected ways to not only capture your audience's attention, but also convey powerful messages about your brand and values. Ready to explore how marketing can creatively harmonize with the environment? Advance with us on this journey.

ENVIRONMENTAL GUERRILLA CAMPAIGNS: CREATING FACILITIES THAT INTERACT WITH THE ENVIRONMENT IN UNEXPECTED WAYS

Environmental guerrilla marketing offers a unique opportunity to connect your brand with your audience in innovative and meaningful ways while emphasizing awareness and respect for the environment. This chapter explores how you can develop campaigns that not only draw attention to your brand, but also promote a positive message of sustainability and caring for the planet.

THE NATURE OF ENVIRONMENTAL GUERRILLA MARKETING

This type of guerrilla marketing uses the natural or urban environment to create installations or experiences that surprise audiences and provoke thought. By doing this, it not only generates visibility for the brand, but also highlights its commitment to environmental issues.

STRATEGIES FOR EFFECTIVE CAMPAIGNS

- **Use sustainable materials:** Ensure that all materials used in your campaign are eco-friendly, biodegradable or recyclable, to minimize the environmental impact.

- **Create powerful messages:** Develop installations that clearly and impactfully communicate the importance of sustainability, encouraging the public to reflect on environmental issues.

- **Interact with the environment creatively:** Think of innovative ways to use the environment around you, whether integrating your installation harmoniously with nature or transforming urban spaces in a way that highlights the interconnection between the environment and society.

- **Promote action:** In addition to drawing attention, encourage specific actions that the public can take to contribute to the environmental cause, whether through social media campaign hashtags, petition signatures or participation in awareness events.

MEASURING SUCCESS

The success of an environmental guerrilla campaign can be measured not only by increasing brand visibility and engagement on social media, but also by the positive impact generated in relation to the public's environmental awareness. Post-campaign evaluations and audience feedback are essential to understanding the reach and reception of your message.

INSPIRING EXAMPLES

Include case studies or examples of brands that have successfully implemented environmental guerrilla campaigns, highlighting the strategies used, challenges faced and results achieved. These examples can serve as inspiration and guidance for developing your own campaigns.

After exploring how guerrilla marketing can be used to foster a deeper connection to environmental issues, the next step is to investigate the world of personalized street art. Discover how to collaborate with local artists to create murals or artistic pieces that not only beautify public space but also convey the essence of your brand. Get ready to dive into the creative possibilities that street art offers for guerrilla marketing. Let's move on to this fascinating territory.

CUSTOM STREET ART

Custom street art is a vibrant and impactful form of guerrilla marketing that allows brands to creatively communicate their messages while contributing to urban aesthetics. This chapter explores how to collaborate with local artists to create murals or art installations that not only capture the public's attention but also reflect your brand's values and personality.

BENEFITS OF STREET ART FOR MARKETING

- **Visibility:** Murals and artistic installations in high-traffic locations ensure great visibility.

- **Emotional connection:** Art has the power to evoke emotions and create deep connections with the public.

- **Community engagement:** Street art projects can engage the local community, creating a sense of belonging and appreciation.

- **Brand image:** Associating your brand with artistic expressions contributes to an innovative and socially responsible image.

PLANNING YOUR ARTISTIC COLLABORATION

- **Artist Choice:** Look for artists whose style and values align with the brand. The authenticity of the partnership is crucial to the success of the project.

- **Concept definition:** Work together with the artist to develop a concept that communicates your message in a subtle but powerful way. The idea must be relevant to both the brand and the local community.

- **Strategic location:** Select locations that not only guarantee visibility, but are also significant to the message you want to convey.

- **Community engagement:** Consider involving the community in the creative process, whether through workshops, design voting or mural reveal events.

- **Promotion and sharing:** Use social media to document the creation process and promote the finished project. This not only increases visibility, but also encourages the public to visit the work and share their experience.

LEGAL AND LOGISTICAL CONSIDERATIONS

- **Permissions and authorizations:** Make sure you obtain all necessary permissions to use your chosen space.

- **Respect for urban space:** Street art should enrich the urban environment, not detract from it. It is essential that the project is in harmony with the location and is respected by the community.

- **Maintenance:** Plan the maintenance of the artwork to ensure it remains in good condition and continues to convey your message effectively.

MEASURING IMPACT

Measure the success of your street art campaign through social media engagement, media coverage, community feedback and, if possible, an increase in awareness and positive brand perception.

After delving into the world of personalized street art, the next chapter will cover how to carry out guerrilla actions at events, whether large fairs, conferences or other gatherings. These strategies can offer unique opportunities to set your brand apart from the competition, without the need to be an official sponsor. Get ready to explore creative techniques to capture the attention of your target audience at events. Shall we proceed?

GUERRILLA ACTIONS AT EVENTS

Presence at events, even when you are not an official sponsor, offers a unique opportunity for brands to stand out. This chapter explores how to carry out guerrilla actions during events, such as fairs, conferences and community gatherings, in a creative and impactful way, ensuring your brand captures the public's attention and imagination.

UNDERSTANDING GUERRILLA ACTIONS AT EVENTS

Guerrilla actions at events focus on creating memorable experiences for attendees without the costs associated with official sponsorship. The idea is to be seen and remembered, taking advantage of the flow of people and the attention focused on the event, but in a way that surprises and delights.

STRATEGIES TO HIGHLIGHT YOUR BRAND

- **Creative interventions:** Use artistic interventions or temporary installations near or around the event to attract attention. This can range from a live performance to an interactive sculpture related to your brand.

- **Strategic gifts:** Distribute gifts or free samples in strategic locations. The goal is to create a buzz around your presence, encouraging attendees to seek out more information about your brand.

- **Mobile advertising:** Consider using bicycles, stickered cars or even drones to promote your brand close to the event, ensuring visibility without being physically present within the official space.

- **Augmented reality:** Use augmented reality applications to create a virtual layer of engagement over the physical event space, allowing attendees to interact with your brand in innovative ways through their smartphones.

PREPARATION AND PLANNING

- **Research:** Know the event, target audience and local

regulations well to ensure that your action is appropriate and effective.

- **Logistics:** Plan all logistical aspects in advance, including transportation, assembly and disassembly of any installation, and the distribution of gifts.

- **Permissions:** Although the idea is to carry out guerrilla action, it is important to ensure that all your activities comply with local laws and regulations.

MEASURING SUCCESS

The success of guerrilla actions at events can be measured by increased social media engagement, media coverage, traffic to the brand's website and, ultimately, the impact on sales or leads generated. Direct feedback from participants can also offer valuable insights.

After exploring how to capture attention during events without being an official sponsor, the next chapter will focus on urban projections. This strategy uses projection technology to create stunning visual advertisements on buildings and other urban structures, offering another powerful way to engage audiences and expand brand visibility. Get ready to light up the city with your message. Let's move forward on this creative journey.

URBAN PROJECTIONS

Urban projections represent a fusion of art, technology and advertising, offering a dynamic platform to capture public attention on a large scale. This chapter explores how to use projection technology to create stunning visual advertisements on buildings and other urban surfaces, transforming ordinary spaces into extraordinary canvases for your brand message.

THE ART OF URBAN PROJECTIONS

Urban projections go beyond traditional marketing, providing an immersive visual experience that can reach a wide audience. They allow brands to tell stories, highlight products or simply create a memorable image associated with innovation and creativity.

PLANNING YOUR URBAN PROJECTION

- **Location selection:** Identify high visibility locations, considering pedestrian traffic and ease of viewing the projection. Public spaces, building facades and monuments are ideal options.

- **Content development:** The projection content must be visually impactful and adapted to the format. Animations, dynamic messages, and interactive elements can increase engagement.

- **Technology and equipment:** The quality of the projection depends on the equipment used. Investing in cutting-edge technology and having a qualified technical team are essential to guarantee the desired clarity and visual impact.

- **Permissions and regulations:** Make sure you obtain all necessary authorizations to carry out the projection, respecting local laws and regulations.

MAXIMIZING IMPACT

- **Interactivity:** Consider incorporating interactive elements, such as allowing the audience to control aspects of the projection via smartphones or react to movements and sounds.

- **Special events:** Aligning projection with local events, holidays or product launches can maximize attention and relevance.

- **Publicity:** Use social networks and other digital platforms to publicize the projection, encouraging the public to visit the location and share the experience online.

MEASURING SUCCESS

The success of an urban projection campaign can be measured by audience engagement, media coverage, social media shares and, ideally, increased brand recognition and interest in the products or services promoted.

After lighting up urban nights with memorable projections, the next step is to explore how distributing guerrilla literature —whether through pamphlets, zines, or booklets—can engage audiences in creative and personal ways. This traditional guerrilla marketing method offers a tangible form of communication, allowing for a direct connection with the audience. Get ready to delve into the art of the printed word and discover how it can be powerfully reintegrated into the digital age. We'll move on to this classic yet timeless tactic in the next chapter.

DISTRIBUTION OF GUERRILLA LITERATURE

The distribution of guerrilla literature reignites the power of the printed word in a digitally dominated era, offering a tangible, personal means of connecting with audiences. This chapter explores how flyers, zines and booklets can be used creatively to communicate your brand message, provoke thought and encourage action.

THE POWER OF THE PRINTED WORD

In a world where digital stimuli are incessant, printed literature draws attention for its physicality and permanence. The ability to hold something real in your hands can create a deeper, more lasting connection with the receiver, making guerrilla literature an effective tool for conveying messages that stick.

CREATING IMPACT CONTENT

- **Clear and direct message:** Content should be concise but powerful, capable of communicating your message effectively in a compact format.

- **Attractive design:** Use a visually stimulating design that attracts the reader and complements the message. Graphic elements, such as illustrations and photographs, can increase appeal.

- **Personalization:** Consider the target audience and personalize content to resonate directly with their interests, needs and values.

- **Strong Call-to- Action (CTA):** Include a clear call to action, encouraging the reader to interact with your brand, whether visiting a website, attending an event or sharing on social media.

EFFECTIVE DISTRIBUTION STRATEGIES

- **Events and strategic locations:** Distribute your literature at events, fairs and other places where your target audience is present. Think outside the box and choose places that can surprise and capture attention.

- **Creative actions:** In addition to direct distribution, consider leaving your materials in unexpected places where they can be discovered, such as cafes, libraries or public transport.

- **Partnerships:** Collaborate with local establishments and groups that share similar values to expand the reach of your distribution.

MEASURING SUCCESS

The impact of guerrilla literature can be assessed through direct audience feedback, increased online traffic (if the material includes digital references), social media engagement, and, depending on the CTA, specific actions taken by the audience.

LEGAL AND ETHICAL CONSIDERATIONS

Respect local regulations on distribution of printed materials and ensure that your campaign is ethical, non-invasive and environmentally conscious, preferring recyclable or eco-friendly materials.

After exploring the impact of printed literature, the next chapter will look at the use of creative poster campaigns. These represent another tangible form of guerrilla marketing, combining art, messaging and strategic location to capture audience attention and communicate effectively. Get ready to dive into the world of posters and discover how this ancient advertising tool can be reinvented to impact modern audiences. Let's move forward.

CREATIVE POSTER CAMPAIGNS

Posters have been a form of visual communication for centuries, evolving from simple advertisements to pieces of art that can provoke, inform and inspire. In the context of guerrilla marketing, creative poster campaigns offer a unique way to capture the public's attention, combining innovative design, impactful messaging and strategic locations to create a striking presence in the urban landscape.

THE POWER OF POSTERS IN GUERRILLA MARKETING

Posters allow a direct and accessible visual expression, capable of reaching many people in public places. They are particularly effective at creating brand awareness and generating conversation, especially when they incorporate creative design elements and provocative or thought-provoking messages.

ELEMENTS OF A SUCCESSFUL POSTER CAMPAIGN

- **Impactful visual design:** The visual aspect is crucial. Use colors, fonts and images that not only attract attention, but also communicate your brand's personality and the essence of the message you want to convey.

- **Clear and concise message:** Given the quick-to-view nature of posters, the message must be direct and memorable. Clever puns, wordplay, or catchphrases can increase message retention.

- **Strategic location:** Choose locations where your target audience is most likely to see the posters and where they will have the greatest impact. High-traffic areas such as public transport stations, plazas and commercial corridors are ideal.

- **Interactivity and engagement:** Consider adding interactive elements such as QR codes for an integrated online campaign, or designs that encourage physical interaction and social media sharing.

EXECUTION AND DISTRIBUTION

- **Permits and legalities:** Check local regulations to ensure poster placement complies with city or region laws.

- **Print quality:** Investing in high-quality materials can increase the durability of posters and ensure they remain visually attractive for longer.

- **Monitoring and maintenance:** Track the response to your campaign and be ready to make adjustments, whether replacing damaged signs or updating the message to maintain interest.

MEASURING IMPACT

The success of a poster campaign can be measured by increased brand awareness, social media engagement (especially if integrated with digital campaigns), audience feedback and, ideally, an increase in sales or direct inquiries.

After exploring visual communication through creative poster campaigns, the next chapter will dive into guerrilla activations in public spaces. These activations are immersive experiences that use the physical environment to engage the audience in a deep and memorable way. Get ready to discover how to transform ordinary spaces into extraordinary settings for unique brand interactions. Let's move on to this engaging and dynamic approach to guerrilla marketing.

GUERRILLA ACTIVATIONS IN PUBLIC SPACES

Guerrilla activations in public spaces are a vibrant and engaging form of guerrilla marketing, designed to transform ordinary locations into extraordinary experiences for audiences. These activations involve creating direct and immersive interactions with the brand, often in unexpected ways, generating impact, conversation and, ideally, a lasting emotional connection with consumers.

PLANNING EFFECTIVE GUERRILLA ACTIVATIONS

- **Creative concept:** The first step is to develop a unique idea that not only catches attention, but is also aligned with the brand identity and the message you want to convey. Originality and relevance to the target audience are crucial.

- **Location Choice:** Identify locations that not only have high traffic from your target audience but are also suitable for the nature of the activation. Consider visibility, accessibility and the possibility of interacting with the space.

- **Audience engagement:** Design the activation to encourage active audience participation. This can range from physical interactions with the installation to actions that promote sharing on social media.

- **Logistics and permissions:** Carefully plan all logistical aspects, including assembly, duration and disassembly of the activation. Additionally, ensure that you obtain all necessary permissions from the responsible bodies.

EXAMPLES OF SUCCESSFUL ACTIVATIONS

- **Interactive artistic installations:** Creations that combine art and technology, inviting the public to interact with the piece in ways that highlight the brand's message.

- **Urban challenges and games:** Activities that challenge the public to participate in games or competitions, often with prizes related to the brand.

- **Live performances:** Using artists or flash mobs to create moments of surprise and enchantment, positively associating these experiences with the brand.

MEASURING IMPACT

The impact of these activations can be assessed through audience engagement during the event, coverage and mentions in the media, increased social media activity related to the brand and, if possible, growth in sales or interest in the products/services promoted.

After exploring the dynamism of activations in public spaces, the next chapter will discuss how vehicles — cars, bicycles, trucks — can be adapted and used in guerrilla campaigns. This strategy not only expands the geographic reach of your actions, but also offers a mobile canvas for creative and impactful messages. Get ready to discover how mobility can be a powerful ally in guerrilla marketing. Let us move forward to explore the unexplored potential of guerrilla actions with vehicles.

GUERRILLA ACTIONS WITH VEHICLES

Using vehicles as mobile platforms for guerrilla marketing can significantly expand the reach of your campaigns, transforming cars, bicycles and trucks into dynamic messengers for your brand. This chapter covers how to adapt vehicles to promote brand messages on the move, creating visual impact and memorable interactions with audiences in different locations.

TRANSFORMING VEHICLES INTO IMPACT MEDIA

- **Visual customization:** Decorating vehicles with the brand's visual identity, including logos, corporate colors and messages, transforms them into mobile advertisements that capture attention wherever they go.

- **Interactivity and technology:** Incorporating interactive elements, such as screens to display videos or sound systems to convey messages, can increase audience engagement. QR code technology can also be used to direct people to the brand's website or social media.

- **Immersive experiences:** Vehicles adapted to offer experiences, such as product tastings or interactive demonstrations, allow the public to experience the brand in a direct and memorable way.

PLANNING YOUR MOBILE CAMPAIGN

- **Itinerary and strategic locations:** Define a route that passes through high-traffic areas of your target audience and consider strategic stops at events or places with a large concentration of people to maximize exposure.

- **Permits and legalities:** Make sure you comply with traffic laws and obtain the necessary permits to avoid mishaps.

- **Security and logistics:** Security is paramount. Ensure vehicles and activations are safe for everyone, including the public and campaign staff.

INSPIRING EXAMPLES

- **Themed food trucks:** Use personalized food trucks to promote food products, offering free samples in different locations.

- **Exhibition cars:** Adapt cars to display new products or technologies in public places, allowing the public to interact directly with the new product.

- **Promotional bicycles:** Use bicycles to distribute gifts or information, taking advantage of their mobility to reach areas difficult to access for larger vehicles.

MEASURING SUCCESS

The success of vehicle campaigns can be measured by increased brand visibility, engagement on social media, media coverage and direct feedback from the public. Analyzing these indicators will help optimize future strategies.

After exploring the potential of guerrilla actions with vehicles, the next step is to delve into guerrilla sensory marketing. This chapter will cover how to create experiences that appeal to the senses, evoking strong emotions and creating a lasting brand memory. Get ready to learn how to engage your audience even more deeply, using the power of the senses. Let's move on to this engaging and memorable approach.

GUERRILLA SENSORY MARKETING

Guerrilla sensory marketing is based on creating experiences that stimulate the audience's senses in innovative and surprising ways, forming a deep emotional connection with the brand. This chapter explores how to apply strategies that appeal to sight, hearing, touch, smell and taste to create lasting memories and strengthen brand identity.

DEEPENING ENGAGEMENT THROUGH THE SENSES

- **Vision:** Use vibrant colors, dynamic lighting or innovative visual projections in public spaces to capture attention and convey impactful messages.

- **Hearing:** Create unique soundscapes or utilize unexpected musical performances to engage audiences in a memorable listening experience that resonates with the essence of the brand.

- **Touch:** Encourage physical interactions with products or facilities that allow the public to experience the quality and unique characteristics of what is being promoted.

- **Smell:** Diffuse aromas that align with your brand or product in specific locations to evoke memories and emotions, influencing consumer perception and behavior.

- **Taste:** Offer tastings of products that surprise the palate, creating a direct and pleasurable experience that will be associated with your brand.

CREATING MEMORABLE CAMPAIGNS

- **Sensory integration:** Combine stimuli from multiple senses to create an immersive, multidimensional brand experience.

- **Strategic location:** Choose locations where you can maximize the sensory impact, considering the context and target audience for the activation.

- **Surprise element:** Surprise intensifies the sensorial experience, making the interaction with the brand unforgettable. Plan unexpected moments that delight your audience.

- **Measuring impact:** Evaluate campaign success through audience engagement, social media sharing, media coverage and direct feedback.

INSPIRING EXAMPLES

- **Olfactory installations:** Perfume brands that create ephemeral gardens in urban areas, allowing people to experience their scents in a natural context.

- **Innovative tastings:** Food companies that use customized vehicles to offer samples of their products in unusual locations, surprising the public with unique flavors.

- **Interactive visual experiences:** Technology brands that use projection mapping and augmented reality in public spaces to create immersive visual experiences.

Moving beyond direct sensory experiences, the next chapter will focus on artistic interventions as a form of guerrilla marketing. These activations use art to communicate brand messages in a subtle and impactful way, creating dialogues with the public in unexpected spaces. Get ready to explore how art can be a powerful tool for conveying brand values and engaging audiences on a deeper level. We will move towards this artistic and expressive approach in the next chapter.

ARTISTIC INTERVENTIONS

Artistic interventions in guerrilla marketing use art to communicate brand messages in subtle but deeply impactful ways. By incorporating art into public or unexpected spaces, brands can create meaningful conversations with the public, conveying values and messages in a creative and memorable way. This chapter explores how these interventions can be employed to enrich brand perception and drive engagement.

WHY ARTISTIC INTERVENTIONS?

- **Emotional connection:** Art has the unique power to evoke emotions and connect with audiences on a personal level, making a brand message more resonant.

- **Visual impact:** Artistic interventions capture attention through their aesthetics, differentiating themselves from the sea of traditional commercial messages.

- **Dialogue with the community:** By positioning art in public spaces, the brand initiates a dialogue with the local community, building relationships and promoting shared values.

STRATEGIES FOR EFFECTIVE IMPLEMENTATION

- **Collaboration with artists:** Partnerships with local artists not only add authenticity to the intervention, but also support the local art scene.

- **Choice of space:** The location of the intervention must be strategically selected to maximize visibility and ensure that the context is aligned with the message.

- **Message integration:** Although the approach is subtle, the brand and its message must be organically integrated into the work, ensuring that the public can make the connection.

- **Public engagement:** Include elements that invite public interaction, whether through direct participation in the creation of the art or through digital platforms for sharing and discussion.

MEASURING IMPACT

The impact of artistic interventions can be assessed through social media engagement, media coverage, community feedback and, if applicable, increased brand awareness and affinity. Qualitative analyses, such as the public's perceptions and feelings towards the brand after the intervention, are also valuable.

INSPIRING EXAMPLES

- **Street art murals:** Murals that tell the story of the brand or that reflect its fundamental values, creating points of cultural and tourist interest.

- **Interactive installations:** Works that require active participation from the public to be completed, symbolizing the collaboration between brand and community.

- **Themed performances:** Artistic events that visually represent the brand's products or services, offering an immersive experience to the public.

After exploring the potential of artistic interventions, the next chapter is dedicated to seasonal guerrilla marketing. This approach leverages holidays, seasons and cultural events to create highly relevant and timely themed campaigns. Get ready to learn how to align your guerrilla marketing strategies with the calendar, maximizing relevance and impact. Let's discover how seasonal occasions can be unique opportunities to engage audiences creatively.

SEASONAL GUERRILLA MARKETING

Seasonal guerrilla marketing capitalizes on specific moments of the year — holidays, seasons, cultural events — to create highly relevant and timely campaigns. This chapter dives into strategies for aligning your guerrilla marketing actions with the calendar, aiming to maximize the impact and resonance of your message with the public.

WHY BET ON SEASONAL?

- **Temporal relevance:** Seasonal campaigns benefit from the public's predisposition to engage with thematic content , increasing receptivity to your message.

- **Opportunities to stand out:** Holidays and cultural events offer a different competitive landscape where creative actions can more easily stand out.

- **Expanded emotional connection:** Festive or seasonal times often carry with them emotions and affective memories, providing an additional layer of emotional connection with the audience.

STRATEGIES FOR SUCCESSFUL SEASONAL CAMPAIGNS

- **Anticipation and planning:** Start planning early to ensure that all aspects of the campaign — from production to execution — are aligned and ready to launch at the ideal time.

- **Customization and personalization:** Tailor your message to reflect the unique characteristics of the season, event or holiday, ensuring the campaign is perceived as relevant and original.

- **Multichannel integration:** Combine actions in the physical world with digital campaigns to expand reach and engagement. Leverage social media to build anticipation before the campaign launches and to amplify the impact during its execution.

- **Measure impact:** Establish clear success metrics before campaign launch. Analyzing social media engagement, media coverage, online traffic and sales can provide valuable insights into campaign performance.

IDEAS FOR INSPIRATION

- **Themed actions in public places:** Use commemorative dates to create interactive installations or performances that can attract public attention and generate spontaneous media.

- **Promotions and special offers:** Align exclusive promotions with the season, encouraging immediate consumer action.

- **Strategic partnerships:** Collaborate with non-competing brands that also seek to engage the same audience during the season, creating joint offers or themed events.

Delving deeper into the essence of guerrilla marketing, the next chapter will address how to encourage and amplify word of mouth in a natural and effective way. This organic form of promotion can be incredibly powerful when combined with creative and memorable campaigns. Get ready to discover strategies that not only generate conversations, but encourage the sharing of positive brand experiences. We will move forward to explore the untapped potential of word of mouth in the context of guerrilla marketing.

WORD OF MOUTH AND GUERRILLA MARKETING

Word of mouth, or "word of mouth" (WoM), is one of the oldest and most effective forms of marketing, based on direct recommendation between people. In the context of guerrilla marketing, stimulating WoM is essential, as creative and memorable campaigns naturally encourage audiences to share their experiences. This chapter explores how to maximize WoM through guerrilla strategies, creating a wave of organic conversations that elevate brand awareness and engagement.

WHY IS WOM POWERFUL?

- **Trust and credibility:** Recommendations from friends, family or acquaintances tend to be more trustworthy than traditional advertising.

- **Expanded reach:** A single shared experience can quickly spread, reaching a vast and diverse audience.

- **Deep engagement:** Personal stories and experiences generate engagement, creating a stronger emotional connection with the brand.

STRATEGIES TO STIMULATE WOM

- **Unique and memorable experiences:** Create campaigns that stand out for their creativity and originality, encouraging people to talk about them.

- **Facilitate sharing:** Make it easy for the public to share their experiences, whether through specific hashtags on social media, dedicated spaces for photos or online tools for sharing stories.

- **Engagement with influencers and community:** Collaborate with influencers who share your brand's values and can act as ambassadors, expanding WoM's reach. Additionally , build an engaged community around your brand, encouraging the sharing of experiences.

- **Rewards and incentives:** Offer incentives for sharing

experiences, such as discounts, free samples or exclusive access to events or products.

MEASURING THE IMPACT OF WOM

Assessing the impact of WoM can be challenging, but some metrics include increased social media engagement, online community growth, sentiment analysis on brand mentions, and of course, an increase in sales or inquiries that can be directly attributed to recommendations..

After understanding the importance and strategies for stimulating word of mouth, the next step is to explore how to measure the overall success of guerrilla marketing campaigns. This chapter will focus on uncovering methods and tools for evaluating the impact and ROI of your guerrilla actions, ensuring you can adjust and optimize future campaigns based on hard data. Get ready to dive into the nuances of performance analysis in the context of guerrilla marketing. We will move forward to unlock the keys to effective measurement.

MEASURING SUCCESS IN GUERRILLA MARKETING

Measuring success is a crucial component of guerrilla marketing, allowing brands to evaluate the impact of their creative campaigns and determine return on investment (ROI). This chapter addresses essential strategies and tools for analyzing the performance of guerrilla actions, facilitating the adjustment and optimization of future initiatives based on concrete insights.

ESTABLISHING CLEAR METRICS

Before launching a campaign, it is vital to define which metrics will be used to evaluate its success. These can vary depending on the specific campaign objectives, including increasing brand awareness, engagement, lead generation or direct sales.

TOOLS AND METHODS FOR MEASUREMENT

- **Social media analytics: Social** media analytics tools can help track brand mentions, engagement, and sentiments expressed by audiences, offering valuable insight into your campaign's impact on the online conversation.

- **Online traffic and conversions:** Use web analytics tools to monitor the increase in traffic to the brand's website, as well as specific conversions that can be attributed to the guerrilla campaign.

- **Surveys and direct feedback:** Conducting surveys or collecting feedback directly from the audience can provide insights into brand perception and the effectiveness of the message conveyed.

- **Media coverage:** Attention from traditional and digital media can be a valuable indicator of campaign success, especially if the goal was to generate buzz or public recognition.

EVALUATING ROI

Determining the ROI of guerrilla marketing campaigns can be complex due to the often indirect nature of the results. However, comparing the total cost of the campaign with the results achieved in terms of audience engagement, media coverage and increased sales can provide an overview of its value.

CHALLENGES IN MEASUREMENT

- **Direct attribution:** It is often challenging to attribute results directly to a specific campaign, especially when multiple channels and tactics are used simultaneously.

- **Measuring long-term impact:** Some benefits of guerrilla campaigns, such as increased brand loyalty, can manifest themselves over time, complicating immediate measurement.

With a firm understanding of how to measure the success of your campaigns, the next step is to develop a concrete action plan to implement effective guerrilla marketing strategies. The next chapter will provide a step-by-step guide to planning, executing, and evaluating guerrilla campaigns, ensuring your brand can capture audience attention in a creative and efficient way. We will move forward to consolidate all of the previously discussed insights and strategies into a cohesive and impactful action plan.

GUERRILLA ACTION PLAN

After exploring the various facets and strategies of guerrilla marketing, it is crucial to consolidate these insights into a detailed and effective action plan. This chapter provides a step-by-step guide to planning, executing, and evaluating guerrilla marketing campaigns, enabling your brand to capture audience attention in a creative and efficient way.

SETTING CLEAR OBJECTIVES

The first step in developing a guerrilla action plan is to establish clear, measurable objectives. This could include increasing brand awareness, promoting a new product or service, engaging a specific audience, or driving sales. Having well-defined objectives is essential to guide all subsequent stages of the plan.

RESEARCH AND SELECTION OF TACTICS

Based on the established objectives, conduct comprehensive research to select the most appropriate guerrilla marketing tactics. Consider factors such as target audience, cultural and social context, and available resources. Tactic selection should align with brand values and campaign objectives.

PLANNING AND LOGISTICS

Each tactic you choose requires a detailed plan that covers all aspects of execution, including:

- **Required resources:** Budget, materials, personnel and technology.

- **Timeline:** Set a detailed timeline, including all phases of the campaign, from preparation to launch and evaluation.

- **Locations:** Choose strategic locations that maximize visibility and impact.

- **Permits and legalities:** Ensure you obtain all necessary permits and comply with local laws.

EXECUTION

The execution of the campaign must follow the established plan precisely, but also be prepared to adapt to unforeseen events. The ability to quickly adjust strategy in response to unexpected challenges or opportunities is a crucial aspect of guerrilla marketing.

EVALUATION AND ADJUSTMENTS

After executing the campaign, it is vital to evaluate its success in relation to the initial objectives, using the metrics and tools defined previously. This analysis should identify strengths, areas for improvement and insights for future campaigns. Be ready to make adjustments based on feedback and results.

DOCUMENTATION AND SHARING OF LEARNINGS

Document the entire process, from planning to execution and evaluation. Sharing learnings, both internally and with partners or through case studies, can provide invaluable value for the professional development of the team and the guerrilla marketing community as a whole.

CONCLUSION

A well-designed guerrilla action plan is the backbone of any successful campaign. By following these steps, your brand will be well-positioned to launch campaigns that not only capture audience attention, but also drive meaningful engagement and contribute to sustainable brand growth. With creativity, careful planning and agile execution, guerrilla marketing can transform the way your brand is perceived and experienced by the public.

As we turn the final page of this journey together, I sincerely hope that the learnings shared here have touched your heart and sparked new perspectives. If this book has brought you any value, I kindly ask that you take a few moments to leave a review on Amazon. Your words not only help me grow and hone my craft, but they also guide other readers in their quests for knowledge and inspiration. Your opinion is a valuable gift, both for me and for the community of readers looking for stories that transform. I sincerely thank you for sharing this journey with me and I hope we can meet again in the pages of a new adventure.

REGINALDO OSNILDO

Hello, I'm Reginaldo Osnildo, author and innovator in the fields of sales, technology, and communication strategies. My background spans from the academic setting, as a professor and researcher at the University of Southern Santa Catarina, to hands-on strategy development at the Catarinense Radio Group. With a PhD in sales narratives and digital convergence, and a Master's in storytelling and social imaginary, I offer my readers a unique blend of theory and practice. My aim is to deliver knowledge in a simple, practical, and didactic language, encouraging direct application in one's personal and professional life.

Yours sincerely

Reginaldo Osnildo

+55 48 991913865

reginaldoosnildo@gmail.com

www.ingramcontent.com/pod-product-compliance
Lightning Source LLC
Chambersburg PA
CBHW070351230526
45471CB00006B/2518